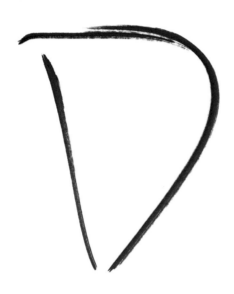

SUPERSTARS OF POKER
TEXAS HOLD'EM

Johnny
"Orient Express"
Chan

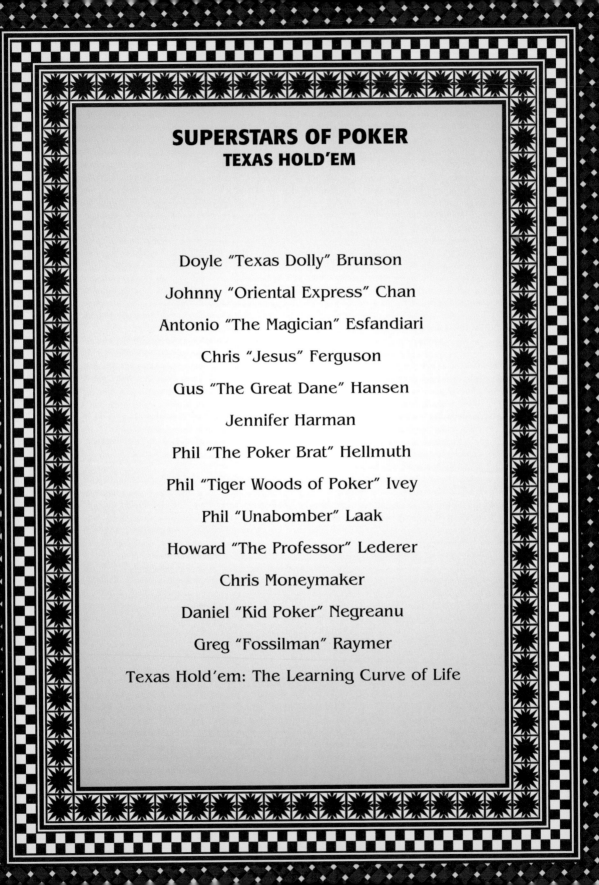

SUPERSTARS OF POKER
TEXAS HOLD'EM

Doyle "Texas Dolly" Brunson

Johnny "Oriental Express" Chan

Antonio "The Magician" Esfandiari

Chris "Jesus" Ferguson

Gus "The Great Dane" Hansen

Jennifer Harman

Phil "The Poker Brat" Hellmuth

Phil "Tiger Woods of Poker" Ivey

Phil "Unabomber" Laak

Howard "The Professor" Lederer

Chris Moneymaker

Daniel "Kid Poker" Negreanu

Greg "Fossilman" Raymer

Texas Hold'em: The Learning Curve of Life

SUPERSTARS OF POKER
TEXAS HOLD'EM

Johnny "Orient Express" Chan

Mitch Roycroft

Mason Crest Publishers

Johnny "Orient Express" Chan

Produced by 21st Century Publishing and Communications, Inc.
Editorial by Harding House Publishing Services, Inc.

MASON CREST PUBLISHERS INC.
370 Reed Road
Broomall, Pennsylvania 19008
(866) MCP-BOOK (toll free)
www.masoncrest.com

Printed in the United States.

First Printing

9 8 7 6 5 4 3 2 1

Library of Congress Cataloging-in-Publication Data

Roycroft, Mitch.
   Johnny "Orient Express" Chan / by Mitch Roycroft.
      p. cm. — (Superstars of poker)
   Includes bibliographical references and index.
   Hardback edition: ISBN-13: 978-1-4222-0224-1
   Paperback edition: ISBN-13: 978-1-4222-0369-9
 1. Chan, Johnny. 2. Poker players—United States—Biography. I. Title.
GV1250.2.C53R685 2008
795.412092—dc22
[B]   2007024793

Publisher's notes:
All quotations in this book come from original sources, and contain the spelling and grammatical inconsistencies of the original text.

The Web sites mentioned in this book were active at the time of publication. The publisher is not responsible for Web sites that have changed their addresses or discontinued operation since the date of publication. The publisher will review and update the Web site addresses each time the book is reprinted.

CONTENTS

INTRODUCTION

by the North American Poker Council

FOR GOOD OR ILL, TEENS LOVE POKER. IT'S BECOME the Friday-night activity of choice for many adolescents. Some adults are pleased, some definitely aren't. So what's the reality?

Well, here are some facts:

- Poker keeps teens occupied in someone's living room or kitchen, rather than out drinking and cruising.

- Poker teaches young adults to pick up on social cues. As they learn to understand "tells," they're gaining insights that help them in a variety of situations.

- Poker develops the portions of the brain that deal with mathematical skills. In today's world where math and the sciences are important to many career paths, those skills are vital.

- Poker helps young adults learn self-control. Kids who have tantrums when things don't go their way don't last long in poker games. Learning to wear a "poker face" helps teens control their up-and-down emotions so they can excel in academic, social, and professional situations.

- Poker gives kids a better understanding of their own mental states. You can't learn self-control without realizing what it is you're controlling. Poker helps adolescents recognize their feelings, which in turn, allows them to get a handle on their emotions.

So if all that's true, why are so many parents and school officials concerned about the new rush of poker-playing teens? In large part, it's because of the moral baggage poker carries; while poker has a long history as a North American pastime, it has an equally long reputation for being shady and sinful. Only recently has poker begun to shake off this reputation and enter the mainstream.

Unfortunately, however, there's good reason for concern when it comes to teens and poker. Here's why: teens who play poker face a real risk of gambling addiction.

So should parents and educators shout a loud, resounding "NO!" when it comes to young adults and poker? Well, that seldom works when it comes to teens; poker is out there, and it's being heavily marketed to the younger generation. A far better choice is to take a look at the realities and assist young adults in developing the skills they'll need to handle poker's challenges wisely.

That's what this series does. It allows teens to learn from the best: the superstars who win time after time. These stars have important life lessons to offer teenagers, and their message is clear: you're not going to have the mental capacity to win if you drink, use drugs, don't get enough sleep, don't eat healthy, or if you allow poker to consume your life.

And isn't that a great message for teens and adults alike to hear?

Chan the Man

♣ ♣ ♣ ♣

JOHNNY CHAN—HIS NAME MEANS POKER. IF YOU ARE going to sit down to a high-stakes poker game with him, you better have experience, you better have guts, you better have brains, and . . . oh yeah . . . you better have money. And one more thing: you better be ready to kiss that money good-bye! Not many people play Johnny Chan and win.

Hall of Famer

In his book, *The Professor, the Banker, and the Suicide King: Inside the Richest Poker Game of All Time*, author Michael Craig described Johnny Chan as a complicated and confusing man:

ALL IN

How To
Win The
BIG ONE
BY 2005 WSOP
CHAMPION
JOE HACHEM

SPECIAL
2006
WORLD SERIES
Preview
Issue

CHAN
THE MAN

Johnny Tops Our Rankings Of The Greatest World Series Players Of All-Time

PLUS:
Doyle Brunson
Ted Forrest

WWW.ALLINMAG.COM
$4.99US $5.99CAN

07>

There is no question that Johnny "Orient Express" Chan has become a dominating force on the professional poker circuit. To many fans, he *is* poker, the name that immediately comes to mind when they hear the word poker. *All In* magazine calls him the Greatest World Series of Poker Player of All Time, and that's no small honor.

> **"Among the top pros and Vegas locals, Chan was a confusing package: phenomenally wealthy or apparently broke, a constant presence or mysteriously absent, patient and talented or impulsive and bored, kind and friendly or cold and angry."**

But as confusing as Johnny Chan can be, one thing is certain: to today's poker fans and players, he is an **icon**, plain and simple. On Friday, September 13, 2002, the Poker Hall of Fame confirmed that iconic status. For the superstitious, Friday the thirteenth is a day to dread, a day that brings bad luck. But Johnny Chan doesn't need to worry about luck; he's got skill. That Friday the thirteenth was a crowning achievement in his career: the Hall of Fame Poker Classic.

The Championship Event was about to begin, and the man nicknamed "The Orient Express" and "The Great Wall of China" was **inducted** into the Poker Hall of Fame. At just forty-five years old, Johnny became the Hall of Fame's twenty-seventh member. Most of the other inductees weren't granted their membership until the final years of their lives, and many were even dead long before the honor was bestowed.

But there was good reason for Johnny's early induction. In 2002, he was in first place on the World Series of Poker (WSOP) all-time money list. He had also won seven WSOP bracelets, just one shy of the record. Hall-of-Famers Johnny Moss and Doyle "Texas Dolly" Brunson shared that record with eight bracelets apiece. But Johnny Moss, who died in 1995, and Doyle, who was approaching seventy at the time, were playing high-stakes poker when Johnny was just a little kid. With more than half his career still before him, it seemed inevitable that Johnny Chan would catch up and perhaps even surpass the older record holders.

Johnny didn't waste too much time with words at the induction ceremony. After all, it was also a tournament, and he was there to play poker. Hall of Fame honors came second to the real prize: victory in the championship. After he and Lyle Berman (who was also inducted into the Hall of Fame that day) received their honors, Johnny stepped to the mic and stated simply, "Shuffle up and deal." The game was on. Johnny didn't win the championship that day, but he will be **immortalized** in the Poker Hall of Fame forever.

In his many years of playing professional poker, Johnny has earned many titles and honors. Among them was his 2002 ranking at the top of the World Series of Poker all-time money list. In this photo, Johnny poses with just some of the millions he has won in his career, along with his signature orange.

One of the reasons for Johnny's success at the poker table is the way he's able to intimidate his opponents. Away from the table, the first Asian to break into poker's top ranks has a reputation for being friendly and funny. He's a definite darling of fans and the media.

Groundbreaker

When looking at the Poker Hall of Fame, a few obvious things stand out about those enshrined there. One is that they are nearly all quite old. Another is that they are all men. Yet another trend is that they are all white—all, that is, except Johnny Chan. Johnny, who is Chinese American, was the first Asian player to break into the top rankings of the high-stakes poker world.

Today, people from all walks of life play high-stakes poker. High-school dropouts, Ph.D.s, computer "geeks," movie stars, newly landed immigrants, Texas cowboys, men, women, young, and old—you will see them all gathered round the tables. But this was not always the case. White men were generally the only people with a seat at high-stakes poker tables, and these men came in two basic forms: extremely wealthy men who didn't mind throwing around their money for some thrills, and rounders—the professional players hungry to suck that money away.

In the last three decades, poker has changed. Now people from all different backgrounds play the game at the highest level. Johnny was one of the first to break in, and he helped pave the way for others. Johnny's success inspired other Asian and minority players, and many have followed in his footsteps.

Poker's Most Famous Man

Johnny Chan is known as a pretty nice guy away from the poker table. At the felt, however, he is intense, with a cold, hard stare, an impenetrable mask-like expression, and an extremely aggressive style. Others sometimes say he is a bully when he plays, but he doesn't mind that reputation. Poker is largely a mental game, and **intimidation** can be an important tool. There aren't many players more intimidating than Johnny.

Away from the poker table, the media likes Chan for his quick wit and flashy designer style. He's probably one of the most famous poker players in the United States. Even if you don't know anything about poker or poker players, there's a very good chance you know Chan's name.

Johnny has been playing poker for more than thirty years, and he's won nearly six million dollars in tournament poker alone. He's won additional untold amounts in cash games, he's been WSOP World Champion twice, and he now shares the record for most WSOP bracelets (in 2005 he brought his total up to ten) with Doyle Brunson and Phil Hellmuth Jr. But it hasn't always been an easy road. Like all professional gamblers, Johnny Chan has struggled. At times it looked like he might not make it at all.

The American Dream

◆ ◆ ◆ ◆

JOHNNY CHAN'S STORY BEGINS FAR FROM POKER, CASINOS, Las Vegas, and all the things that define his life today. His life began half a world away in a different country with a different way of life. He was born in 1957 in Guangzhou, China, a huge city with the third-largest population in the country.

Coming to America
Johnny's parents wanted a better life for their children, and they hoped to find that life in America. When Johnny was nine years old, his family

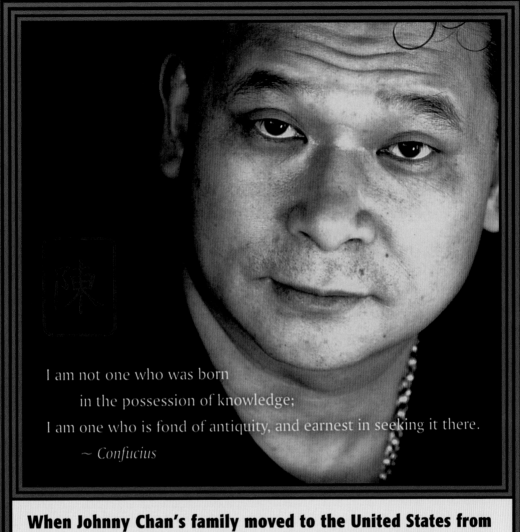

I am not one who was born

in the possession of knowledge;

I am one who is fond of antiquity, and earnest in seeking it there.

~ *Confucius*

When Johnny Chan's family moved to the United States from China in the late 1960s, they wanted a better life for their young children. Though poker was probably not what his parents had in mind for a career choice, the game has brought the best things to Johnny and the members of his family.

moved to the United States and settled in Phoenix, Arizona. Later, they moved to Houston, Texas.

In an interview with Steve Hirano for Goldsea.com, Johnny remembered how difficult those early years were:

"I spoke zero English. In the whole school there was only one other Asian. The other kids tell you something, you don't know what they're talking about. Sometimes they laugh at you, and you don't know what they're laughing about. They yell at you and you don't know what they're yelling about. That was tough."

Johnny's parents worked tirelessly to make a life in America. They opened a restaurant and prepped their son for the business. As a teenager, Johnny worked long hours at the restaurant and prepared to follow in his parents' footsteps. But something else intervened.

Discovering His Passion

Like all teenagers, Johnny loved having fun with his friends. When he wasn't working, he was usually at the bowling alley. Bowling was his favorite pastime, and he was good—good enough to make a lot of money since he and his friends always bet on the games.

One night at the bowling alley, Johnny joined a poker game, and it lit an instant passion. In an interview for Pokerzone TV, he fondly remembered those first games:

"I used to play with friends for nickels and dimes. . . . If you won 20 bucks you'd have to buy everyone breakfast! But it wasn't about the winning or losing, it was about being among friends, having a good time and learning the game."

Things got more serious when Johnny moved up to the underground games held in the back of his family's restaurant. He was soon doubling his restaurant earnings at the poker table.

Everyone realized Johnny had a special talent. As he improved his skills, he became too dangerous for the game. The other players decided to oust the young gun; he was emptying their pockets too often. They told Johnny they'd cancelled the game. Suspicious, Johnny showed up at the restaurant on the regular poker night, only to discover the players were there. The writing was on the wall. He wasn't welcome anymore.

Viva Las Vegas

Johnny was sixteen and looking for some action. Where better to look than Las Vegas? Of course it was illegal for him to play; he was underage. But that didn't stop him from flying there with some friends and finding a game. In an interview with Paul Cheung for *Inside Edge* magazine, Johnny explained what happened in his first trip to the city of his dreams:

Life for the teenaged Johnny Chan was a lot like other teens living in Texas. He and his friends loved to get together and bowl; and Johnny was good at it. But then he discovered poker, and he quickly showed even seasoned players that he had a definite talent for the game.

The big poker games are generally held in casinos. One of the most famous casinos in Las Vegas, Nevada, is the Golden Nugget. Many poker players have made—and lost—fortunes within those walls. The Golden Nugget's poker room was the scene of one of Johnny's earliest triumphs as a poker player.

"I blew my $2,500 in the first few hours. Then I walked downtown to the Golden Nugget and I discovered this poker room. . . . I watched those guys play and I said to myself, 'I can beat those guys.' I got my MasterCard, paid about 15% juice [interest] and, from that $300, I went up to $30,000 in about a week.**"**

It was more money than most people made in a year, a dream come true. Johnny felt invincible. But his dream turned into a nightmare when he blew every cent at the blackjack and roulette tables. Broke, he headed back to Houston. He didn't give up poker—but he didn't tell his parents what happened in Las Vegas either.

After high school, Johnny entered the University of Houston's hotel and restaurant management program. But the poker itch was always present. When he turned twenty-one, he decided to scratch that itch. Johnny dropped out of school and returned to Las Vegas to become a professional gambler. In his *Inside Edge* interview, he explained that he was going against his family's wishes, but he was following his dream:

> **"[My parents are] old-fashioned Chinese. They didn't want me to gamble. They wanted me to run their family restaurant, and that was going to be the foundation for the rest of my life. I didn't want to do that, so I decided to move to Vegas. When I got here, I felt like I'd died and gone to heaven. I love this town!"**

POKER HISTORY

The history of poker is thought to have evolved over more than ten centuries from various games. More than a thousand years ago, the Chinese emperor Mu-tsung is reported to have played "domino cards" with his wife on New Year's Eve. Egyptians in the twelfth and thirteenth centuries used a form of playing cards, and in the sixteenth century, Persians were using cards to play a variety of betting games. A French game named "Poque" and a German game named "Pochen" were popular in the seventeenth and eighteenth centuries; both developed from the sixteenth-century Spanish game called "Primero." French colonists imported the game to the "New World" when they arrived in Canada and New Orleans. After America became a nation, poker spread from the state of Louisiana up the Mississippi River on riverboats—and then throughout the whole country. During the Wild West period of U.S. history, a saloon with a poker table could be found in just about every town from coast to coast. The game was extremely popular during the Civil War, when the soldiers of both armies passed their time with hands of cards.

The Orient Express

♠ ♠ ♠ ♠

IF JOHNNY THOUGHT HE'D GET RICH QUICK IN VEGAS, HE was sorely mistaken. He was soon selling his jewelry and other personal possessions just to stay in the game. Johnny learned what many people learn about Vegas: for all its beautiful fountains and dazzling lights, it's designed to suck people dry.

Too Much Gamble

Johnny had a big problem. He wasn't just a poker player, he was a real gambler. He loved action—all kinds of action—and he spent a lot of time at game tables and bookies. In poker he had a significant edge. He

Despite his earlier success at the Golden Nugget casino in Las Vegas, Johnny Chan soon learned that life as a professional poker player was anything but easy. But Johnny was determined to make it, and he sold personal belongings to stay in the game. In time, his perseverance paid off—in a big way.

had the excellent skills, the smarts, and the guts. But casino games are an entirely different story because they aren't about skills. Instead, they are about odds, and the odds are always stacked against you. If you play the games long enough, you will certainly lose. There's no doubt about it; that's just the way the numbers are. That's why casinos make billions of dollars a year.

Johnny couldn't stay away from the games tables and betting. He just plain liked to gamble. It's a quality he admitted to *Inside Edge* he has never lost:

> **"I've always had leaks. I bet sports, on the fight, used to shoot craps, baccarat. I'm a gambler. I know poker is the only one I can have an edge on—in fact, I knew that 30 years ago—but I still do all those other things."**

In those early years, Johnny did those other things way too much and found himself broke over and over again. And the "leaks" crept into his poker game as well. When playing his A game, he could easily take other players down, but no one can play his best game all the time. Phil Ivey, one of the most successful poker players today, explained in an interview to *Card Player* magazine why many good poker players don't win:

> **"Some people might be very good poker players, but I'll end up winning because I'm a better gambler. . . . I know when to quit, when to keep playing all night, when my opponent's off his game, and when I'm off my game. . . . That's all part of gambling. People say, 'Oh, I'm not gambling when I'm playing poker.' Yes, you are. But you've got to know how to do it."**

In those early years, Johnny *didn't* know how to do it. He had too much gamble for his own good. Years later, Doyle Brunson explained that back in the early days, Johnny was just too much of a loose cannon to be his best:

So what makes a successful poker player? According to poker great Phil "the Tiger Woods of Poker" Ivey (shown in this photo), the best players know certain things—and that doesn't mean taking unnecessary risks. Phil means the ability to know when to throw in the towel, being honest with himself about when his A game isn't working.

> **"Johnny was a hot-headed kid with some talent. But he didn't know when to keep his temper under control or know when to quit playing."**

Making the Change

Unlike a lot of professional gamblers, Johnny realized his faults early on and vowed to fix them. He calmed down and did an about-face in

Johnny knew that he had to tame his temper—and his lifestyle— if he wanted to be successful at professional poker. He worked hard, started eating better, and took better care of himself. Soon, his vow paid off, and Johnny started making it to final table after final table. He quickly became a fan favorite.

his lifestyle. The four-pack-a-day smoker threw his cigarettes in the trash. He stopped drinking alcohol. He started exercising and eating right. He began bringing an orange to the poker table—the scent helped ward off the smell of cigarettes—and it became his trademark. Rumors circulated that it was a powerful good-luck charm, and imitators followed with their own lucky fruit. The changes paid off. Johnny became unstoppable.

Johnny was on fire. He played poker sixty hours a week, and he couldn't have been happier. He wasn't at the top of the poker ladder yet, but he was climbing and having tons of fun. In his Pokerzone TV interview he remembered those early years when nothing was better than sitting down to a poker game, win or lose:

> **"When I first moved to Vegas in [the] late 70s, early 80s, I loved the game so much, I didn't ever want to go home. If they had a bed in the poker room, I would have slept there, so I could just wake up and play."**

Rung by rung, Johnny ascended, learning from his mistakes, mastering the game, and gaining a reputation. He concentrated on cash games and then branched out into tournament poker. For many professional players, cash games are where you grind out a living. Tournaments are where you win recognition and respect.

Domination

Johnny began his tournament domination by winning Bob Stupak's America's Cup of Poker in 1982 and again in 1983. He earned his famous nickname there by rushing into the tournament like a freight train, sending thirteen out of sixteen players to the rails in just over half an hour. From that day forward, he'd be called the "Orient Express."

In 1985, Johnny had his next significant tournament win when he conquered the $1000 Omaha event at Amarillo Slim's Superbowl of Poker. The win was nice, but it was small fry compared to what would happen a few months later. At that time, there was really only one poker tournament in the world that mattered: the WSOP. Johnny Chan was about to make his mark.

The WSOP began in 1970. It's still the largest and most respected tournament on earth. Benny Binion, owner of Binion's Horseshoe casino in Las Vegas, invited seven men to square off for the World Champion title. They were Johnny Moss, "Amarillo Slim" Preston, "Sailor" Roberts, Walter "Puggy" Pearson, Crandell Addington, Carl Cannon, and Doyle "Texas Dolly" Brunson. Those men are now all legends, and the tournament carries on, every year getting bigger, with more players and larger prizes.

Today the World Series consists of preliminary events followed by the $10,000 No Limit Hold'em World Championship. Winners receive huge prize money and gold bracelets. For many people, those **coveted** bracelets are the ultimate sign of success in the high-stakes poker world. In 1985, Johnny took home his first bracelet when he won the $1000 Limit Hold'em Event. It came with a $171,000 prize, and the knowledge that he was becoming one of the best poker players around.

Crowned the Best

In 1987, Johnny was back at the WSOP and going for the big one: the $10,000 No Limit Hold'em World Championship. One hundred fifty-two people fought for the prize, but the Orient Express ran them down. When the dust cleared, Johnny Chan was the last man standing. He was World Champion and $625,000 richer.

The 1988 WSOP was déjà vu. Chan steamrolled over the competition and made it to the final two. In the end, he was heads-up (meaning one-on-one) against Erik Seidel. It looked like it was all over for Johnny. Johnny lost a $1.2 million pot—the largest in recorded poker history—to put him way behind in chips. But Johnny fought back, in the end deftly luring Erik into a trap. A few subtle, **feigned** signs of weakness from Johnny, and Erik waltzed all-in (bet all of his chips). But Johnny had the cards, and the tournament was over. He was World Champion for the second year in a row. Ten years later, that final hand would be immortalized when a clip of it was shown in the movie *Rounders*, starring Matt Damon and Edward Norton. Johnny would also make a cameo appearance in the film.

No one has won consecutive championships since Johnny's 1988 win, and because the field has grown so much, most people think it will never be done again. But if two in a row wasn't impressive enough,

The very first World Series of Poker featured only seven specially invited players. Among them were Thomas "Amarillo Slim" Preston (left in cowboy hat) and Doyle "Texas Dolly" Brunson (far right, in glasses), shown in this photo from the 1970s. From the seven players in the first tournament, the series has grown in popularity—and purse size—each year.

Johnny nearly made it three in 1989. That year, Los Angeles Lakers' owner and poker enthusiast Jerry Buss promised Johnny his NBA championship ring if Johnny could win the championship for a third straight year.

The Rivalry Begins

The final table of the 1989 WSOP championship came down to Johnny Chan and an upstart kid from Madison, Wisconsin, Phil Hellmuth Jr. Johnny had an amazing run, but in the end, Phil claimed the prize. It

It was Johnny's turn to taste success at the World Series of Poker in 1987. He held off one hundred and fifty-one other players to come out on top when the last card was turned at the final table. Besides a $625,000 payoff and a nice trophy, Johnny won a coveted World Series of Poker bracelet.

was the start of what is now perhaps the poker world's biggest rivalry: Johnny Chan vs. Phil Hellmuth Jr. The battle still rages today, and in an interview for *Bluff* magazine, Johnny talked about the championship loss that started it all:

> **"I hate to lose to Phil [Hellmuth]. But, unfortunately, I did. I didn't play my best. I shouldn't have put all my money in there with A-7. I was tired. We'd played for three and a half days straight. . . . I didn't get enough rest. I was burned out."**

It's a loss Johnny has never quite gotten over. Later in the interview he said he let a once-in-a-lifetime opportunity slip away. He still thinks about that losing hand and regrets the way he played it:

> **"I overplayed that hand and it cost me my third championship in a row. I'm the only person ever who had that opportunity—no one in history has ever come that close, and I don't think anyone ever will. There's too many people in the running now. I blew it, but what can you do?"**

Most people, however, don't consider Johnny's second-place finish "blowing it" at all. Steve Hirano's Goldsea.com article quotes Doyle Brunson on Johnny's accomplishments:

> **"You could play a million years and it would never happen again. Not only did Johnny win it twice and come in second, he won two other tournaments in between. He won four big tournaments in a row and came in second in the next one. It was very extraordinary."**

Quest to Be the Best

Phil's 1989 victory started a WSOP bracelet race that continues to this day. Both men wanted WSOP supremacy, but to achieve it, they'd

By 1989, there was a rivalry building among poker players to see who could win the most World Series of Poker bracelets. Thick in the middle of the three-man race was the Orient Express (fourth from left in this 2006 photo). Phil Hellmuth Jr. (fifth from left) and Doyle Brunson (left) fought Johnny for the bracelet lead.

have to battle a third man as well: Doyle Brunson. When their bracelet race began, Phil only had one, Johnny had three, but Doyle Brunson had seven.

In 1994, Johnny won the $1500 Seven Card Stud event, bringing his WSOP bracelet count to four. His fifth bracelet came in 1997 in $5000 Deuce to Seven Draw. But unfortunately for Johnny, Phil had been busy racking up bracelets of his own, and he was doing it faster than his rival. In 1997, Phil won his sixth bracelet, surpassing Johnny in the bracelet count.

Seeing the young guns closing in, Doyle won an eighth bracelet the next year, tying the legendary Johnny Moss for the record and distancing himself from his pesky followers. It took until 2000 for Johnny to win his sixth bracelet, this time in $1500 Pot Limit Omaha. In 2001, Phil answered back with a seventh bracelet. In 2002, Johnny won the $2500 No Limit Hold'em Gold Bracelet Match Play event, earning his seventh bracelet. That year, he was also inducted into the Poker Hall of Fame, an honor that has not been bestowed on Phil—at least not yet.

WHEN GAMBLING IS A MENTAL ILLNESS

The American Psychiatric Association's most recent version of the *Diagnostic and Statistical Manual* (DSM-IV-R), defines a mental illness called pathological gambling as behavior that meets at least five of the following criteria: *Preoccupation*; the individual has frequent thoughts about gambling experiences, whether past, future, or fantasy. *Tolerance*; as with drug tolerance, the individual requires larger or more frequent wagers to experience the same "rush." *Withdrawal*; restlessness or irritability is associated with attempts to cease or reduce gambling. *Escape*; the person gambles to improve mood or escape problems. *Chasing*; the individual tries to win back gambling losses with more gambling. *Lying*; the person tries to hide the extent of his or her gambling by lying to family, friends, or therapists. *Loss of control*; the person has unsuccessfully attempted to reduce gambling. *Illegal acts*; the individual has broken the law in order to obtain gambling money or recover gambling losses. *Risked significant relationships*; the person continues to gamble despite risking or losing a relationship, job, or other significant opportunity. *Bailout*; the individual turns to family, friends, or another third party for financial assistance as a result of gambling. *Biological basis*; the person has a lack of certain brain chemicals that make him or her crave the emotional rush created by gambling.

Psychiatrists point out that not all "problem gamblers" are addicted, nor do they qualify for a label of pathological gambling; they are not in the grip of an uncontrollable and unhealthy compulsion to gamble, and yet gambling still interferes with their lives. Someone who gambles more than she can afford, for example, and then gambles more to retrieve her losses only to lose still more, has a serious problem—but she is not necessarily addicted to gambling.

Poker Revolution

♥ ♥ ♥ ♥

IN 2002, BIG THINGS WERE HAPPENING FOR JOHNNY CHAN.
He was riding high as the newest member of the Poker Hall of Fame. Big things were happening for the game of poker as well. High-stakes poker was about to become the television industry's newest darling, and the game's biggest players were about to become celebrities.

A History in the Shadows

For most of its history, poker was a backroom game, played in the shadows. Its players weren't celebrities. In fact, they avoided the spotlight. Too much attention could be dangerous. Gambling was illegal almost

As a new century began, poker was experiencing growth it had never before seen. Its popularity grew by leaps and bounds. One of the "poster kids" for the game was Johnny Chan, posing here with *Top Pair* magazine, which featured a story about the amazing success of the "Orient Express."

everywhere. Furthermore, professional poker players carried lots of cash, and robberies were common. In addition, playing poker wasn't exactly the most respectable pastime, and a strong criminal element surrounded the high-stakes poker world.

Rounders, even those who carefully walked the legal lines, operated in a dangerous world. Cheating was common. Being cheated could mean losing everything. Being found cheating, or even suspected of cheating, was a sure ticket to a beating, and sometimes even death. Even in a completely honest game, you could still lose everything. The stress was incredible, tempers often flared, and violence could erupt.

Doyle Brunson began his career as a rounder in the 1950s. Today he's considered the "godfather" of poker, and he still plays with the best of the best. When he started playing, there weren't casinos or poker rooms with world-class security. It was a rough world. He faced danger and saw people get killed. In his book *Super System*, he described just one of the times he was robbed, something professional gamblers could expect to experience more than once:

> **"I could hear the pale honking of a car far behind us on the highway. The sound grew closer. Finally I saw another car behind me. . . . The other car came alongside ours and stayed there for several seconds. . . . Suddenly, [the driver] rolled his window down and pointed a large gun at my head. . . . It was a fast hijacking. No one got hurt. Red and I were tied up and left to grovel in the mud of a nearby field. . . . They'd got all our money except $550, which was kept in the glove compartment for emergencies."**

Obviously, poker playing was risky business.

Evolution Under Way

In the 1970s, things began to change for poker and its players. Legal gambling hotspots, like Las Vegas, grew. Casinos with poker rooms offered safe places to play. Cheating became less common and harder to pull off. Tournaments like the WSOP brought **legitimacy** to the

PRINT/ONLINE DIGITAL **MAGAZINE**

♠ AMERICAN POKER PLAYER

APPMagazine.com July/August 2006 $4.95

COVER STORY

High Stakes Poker: GSN Raises the Stakes for Poker on Television

Gavin Smith
WPT Player of the Year

The Bicycle Casino
The Gem of the West Coast

There is More to Life
Than No-Limit: Part III
By Susie Isaacs

PULL OUT
POKER GUIDE
FOR WINNING
HANDS

Poker has come a long way from the days when it was played by rounders who dodged criminals and the law to make a living. One of the best of the rounders was Doyle "Texas Dolly" Brunson. Doyle has been a part of poker history and continues to be a force on the circuit.

game. Television broadcasts of tournaments, even with low ratings, gave poker a public face.

As the next step in poker's evolution to respectability, poker books appeared on store shelves. It all started with Doyle Brunson. He became the first poker player to win one million dollars in tournament play, and he published a book called *How I Made $1,000,000 Playing Poker*. That **piqued** people's interest. The prospect of becoming a millionaire by playing a game was attractive to say the least. The book

As poker's popularity has increased, so has the number of books and videos available to help the novice improve his game. Johnny wrote *Play Poker Like Johnny Chan*, much to the delight of his fans. In this photo from 2005, Johnny poses (holding his book) with fellow poker champ Chris Moneymaker (right) and a guest.

was later republished under the title *Super System*. Today, many people call it "the Bible of Poker."

More how-to books followed. Then, starting in the late eighties, computers made their mark. There was no Internet as we know it today, but the first networks were rapidly growing. People could play poker in text-only chat rooms. Within a decade, the Internet changed everything about poker. People were playing online in droves, and some were making their way to the WSOP. Every year, the field at the World Series grew. The main event had seven players in 1970, seventy-three players in 1980, 194 players in 1990, and 512 players in 2000. But that was nothing compared to what would happen next. The new millennium would be a new dawn for poker.

Poker's New Dawn

Despite poker's increased popularity, in the year 2000, most professional players were still unknown to the general public. Johnny Chan was one of the few players who already had celebrity status. A lot of that status was due to *Rounders*, which had premiered in 1998. It wasn't a huge box office smash, but it gained a cult following. In his *Bluff* magazine interview, Johnny talked about how important he felt the movie was to poker:

> **❝*Rounders* put poker on the map. People went to see the movie and suddenly they wanted to be like Johnny Chan and win the World Series in Las Vegas. I got recognized a lot more after *Rounders*, and it helped poker a great deal.❞**

The popularity of everything to do with poker had indeed grown by leaps and bounds. But one thing hadn't changed: television poker was as boring as ever. Despite the success of *Rounders* and some other poker films, poker on television was **stagnant**, with little interest and low ratings. By 2002, however, that too was about to change.

A television producer named Steven Lipscomb had been watching poker's popularity increase for years. By the new millennium, he was convinced that high-stakes poker would be television's next big thing. In 2002, he started a series of fully televised poker tournaments called the World Poker Tour.

Poker has also caught the eye of the movie world. Several films have called on the poker pros to be consultants, making certain that everything poker related is depicted accurately. Here, Doyle Brunson (second from right) and Johnny Chan (far left) are on the set of the film *Lucky You*.

The first episodes aired on the Travel Channel in 2003. They were an instant success, quickly becoming the highest-rated program in Travel Channel history. Poker itself would soon be the third-most popular sport on television. Entrance to the WSOP swelled as well. In 2003, 839 players entered the main event, and first prize grew to $2.5 million.

A Historic Battle at the WSOP

The 2003 WSOP was historic for another reason. That year records were smashed. Johnny and Phil were both within striking distance of

Doyle's eight bracelets. It was perhaps just the motivation Doyle needed. On April 23rd, Doyle won his ninth bracelet while the two younger men still sat at seven. But Johnny and Phil were ready to take Doyle on.

Less than a week after Doyle's win, Johnny won the $5000 No Limit Hold'em event for his eighth bracelet. Approximately one week later, he tied Doyle for the record when he took down the $5000 Pot Limit Omaha event for a ninth bracelet. But in the race with Phil, the victory was short lived. The grit from Doyle and Johnny's dust must have been too much for Phil to swallow, because he too won his eight and ninth bracelets at the tournament.

After the fireworks of 2003, the 2004 WSOP was a bit disappointing for the bracelet leaders; all three went home empty-handed. That changed in 2005. Johnny finally cracked Doyle's record when he claimed victory in the $2500 Pot Limit Hold'em event, earning his tenth WSOP bracelet. The final table was a showdown between ever-composed Johnny and ever-boisterous pro Phil Laak.

The action at the final table was so intense, and Phil Laak's behavior so bizarre, that ESPN decided the Johnny Chan/Phil Laak showdown needed to be caught on film. In an article for *Poker Player Newspaper*, author Nolan Dalla reported how the final moments of the game unfolded:

> **❝Johnny Chan may have seen everything in his 23 years as a pro, but he had certainly not witnessed the equivalent of Phil 'Unabomber' Laak playing the role of circus clown, crazed lunatic, and grand shaman all wrapped up in a single, seemingly disturbed, poker player. Chan sat stoically, while Laak bounced around the final table like Jackson Pollack painting a canvas. He darted back and forth around Chan, the dealer, and the Tournament Director—often in the middle of hands. . . . Like a deranged madman, Laak had the audience (and occasionally Chan, too) in stitches. No one would have thought there was about 150 grand riding on the outcome.❞**

Some people have claimed that Johnny is a bully when he plays. Even more people have stated that Phil "Unabomber" Laak is just plain weird. Though some might think he uses his trademark hoodie and sunglasses to intimidate his opponents, Phil has said they help him from showing his "tells" to the other players.

The entertainment ended, however, when Phil, holding a king and a jack, went all-in. When the last card hit, Phil's best hand was a pair of jacks. Johnny turned over his hole cards: a pair of queens. The show was over. The record was his, but not for long. Four days later, Doyle won his own tenth bracelet. (Phil Hellmuth wouldn't rejoin the men at the top until the 2006 WSOP, where he won a tenth bracelet of his own.)

Sharing the Wealth

There were no bracelets at the 2006 WSOP for Johnny. But the tournament brought him an accomplishment of a different kind. He had been mentoring television-producer-turned-poker-player Jamie Gold. Jamie's performance in the WSOP main event proved Johnny wasn't just a great player; he was also a great teacher.

A record 8,773 players entered the main event, more than ten times the number just three years ago. Johnny Chan was knocked out of play on the first day, but his **protégé**, Jamie Gold played on. After a grueling week of nearly nonstop action, Jamie was the last player standing. He collected a whopping $12 million, the largest cash prize in sports or television history.

Jamie Gold is now clearly a great poker player, and he has nothing but respect for the man who helped get him to his world champ status.

WHO IS THE UNABOMBER?

Phil Laak was born in Dublin, Ireland, but he grew up in Massachusetts, where he went to the University of Massachusetts for a degree in mechanical engineering. His first love was backgammon, but in 1999, he began playing poker, and eventually, exploded into the world of poker stardom in 2003. His unique personality and antics made him a favorite with spectators and helped propel him to fame. Phil is famous for jumping around the table, doing push-ups in the middle of a tense game, or getting down on his knees next to the dealer, waiting for the first glimpse of the next card to be dealt. Phil's face was as expressive as his body, which isn't a good thing in poker; that's where the term "poker face" came from, after all, since the best players don't reveal what's in their hands with their expressions. To compensate for the fact that his face was an open book, Phil began wearing a hooded sweatshirt and sunglasses. He found that this attire had the added advantage of intimidating his opponents, and it soon became his signature look. Because he looked like the Unabomber, he was awarded the nickname. But there's a whole lot more to Phil than just bizarre behaviors and a hoodie. He's a brilliant poker player who loves to study game theory, and his success owes as much to his intelligence as it does to luck.

In an interview with Erik Sylven for PokerListings.com, Jamie said he won't be ready to challenge his teacher any time soon:

> **"Johnny Chan . . . is one of the great masters of poker. I've got one bracelet and he has ten. Ten bracelets is an amazing accomplishment and it reflects the quality of player that Johnny Chan is. Johnny and I are still close and I hope to continue to learn from him."**

One of the traditions of the professional poker circuit is the practice of veteran players helping out younger ones. Johnny is continuing the tradition as he mentors Jamie Gold of California. And Johnny must be doing a great job: Jamie won the WSOP No Limit Texas Hold'em main event in 2006!

Poker Superstar

Winning WSOP bracelets and mentoring a World Champion are by no means the only accomplishments Johnny has had since the start of the poker boom. In 2005, he played in the first season of Fox Sports Net's **elite** *Poker Superstars Invitational Tournament.* Only eight players were invited: Barry Greenstein, Doyle Brunson, Howard Lederer, David "Chip" Reese, T.J. Cloutier, Phil Ivey, Johnny Chan, and Gus Hansen. At one point Johnny was down to only $20,000 worth of chips (out of $3.2 million worth in play), but he staged an incredible comeback and finished second to Gus Hansen.

In the second season of the *Poker Superstars Invitational Tournament,* Johnny redeemed himself. In the grand final, he defeated Todd Brunson. In the tournament's third season, however, Johnny came up a bit short, finishing fifth in the championship round.

In 2007, Johnny recaptured a bit of glory when he won the "World Series of Poker Champions" episode on NBC's *Poker After Dark.* He beat Doyle Brunson, Chris Moneymaker, Chris Ferguson, Jamie Gold, and Carlos Mortensen for the win. He hopes 2007 will be big for him in another way. At the WSOP, he plans to pick up his eleventh bracelet and overtake his record rivals.

The One and the Only

♣ ♣ ♣ ♣

JOHNNY IS STILL AN UNDISPUTED KING OF THE POKER world. And yet, these days, fans don't see quite as much of him at the poker table. Today, Chan is almost too busy to play poker. Becoming a famous poker player opened a lot of other doors, and he's now a businessman.

The Doors of Opportunity

As Johnny's poker greatness turned into celebrity, the doors of opportunity flew open. There have been book deals, movie offers, a restaurant business, and so much more. The opportunities, however, have a price. Johnny explained to *Inside Edge* that as his business

chanpoker.net

Michael Jordan (left) and Scottie Pippin (right) are big poker fans—and big fans of Johnny Chan. Johnny's fans come from all walks of life and from all over the world. As he expands his influence beyond the poker world, so does the number of people he draws into his fold.

world has grown, his poker life has shrunk, and some joy has been sucked from the game:

> **"Nowadays, I'm so busy promoting my book. I have restaurants. I'm working on opening a casino right as we speak. I own a piece of *Rounders* magazine. I have Chanpoker.com coming out soon. . . . There are more business opportunities than ever, so I don't have as much time to play poker any more. I don't have the feeling any more. The heartbeats aren't there. It's just another day at the office!"**

As the number of Johnny's championships grew, so did the number of business opportunities that became available to the Orient Express. He writes books, owns a restaurant, works on films, and even has his own invitational poker tournament. He also has a large, close family. No wonder he has a hard time finding time to play poker these days!

In addition to being a poker player and businessman, Johnny is also a family man. He has six children, and unlike a lot of poker professionals, he doesn't shield them from poker. He even sounded encouraging of their interest when he talked about one of his daughters with *Inside Edge* magazine:

> **"My daughter, she's very good. She's only 13 years old and wins a [poker] tournament every day."**

The Killer Instinct

Johnny, however, isn't ready to let the next generation take over yet. He may not be the young, hot-headed kid of the old days, but there's still a lot of fight in Johnny Chan. He told *Inside Edge* that, despite a shifting career focus and less time to play, he's still passionate and driven to win:

> **"I'll always have the killer instinct. If you stay in the game and you're not motivated, you don't belong there. So any time I sit in a game, I want to win."**

Thoughts on the Competition

Sometimes Johnny's killer instinct, however, can look like poor sportsmanship. His attitude toward his rivals, particularly toward Hellmuth, can be downright scornful. In his interview for *Inside Edge*, Johnny refused to give Phil too much credit for his WSOP accomplishments:

> **"When you play 85% [of] tournaments compared with my 15% and you only have nine bracelets, what do you think? If I played that many, I'd have at least 20. I'd win a bracelet every year, no question about it."**

Phil is by no means the only player Johnny has made disparaging comments about. Nevertheless, he's not without his own heroes. He's named Doyle Brunson and Phil Ivey as the top players in the world (along with himself of course). Furthermore, in his *Bluff* magazine interview, he talked about the player he most admires:

BLUFF

The Thrill of Poker

HOLLYWOOD CELEBRITIES
Battle on the Felt

CIRCLE OF OUTLAWS:
Marcel Luske's Team of Deadly Assassins

PLUS:
John Elway Gets into the Game, Caesars New Poker Room and More

PHIL HELLMUTH

TALKS ABOUT DODGING BULLETS, CELEBRITY STATUS AND BEING THE BEST

$4.99 US/$6.99 CAN
March 2006

0 3>

7 87838 96978 4

America's #1 Poker Publication

Johnny's competition with Phil Hellmuth Jr. has gone on for many years. Johnny has downplayed Phil's accomplishments, saying he'd have twice as many bracelets if he played as much as Phil does. But Johnny's not alone in his criticism of the "Poker Brat." Some other players find Phil's antics rude and annoying.

Despite the fact that some of his opponents call him a bully at the table, most professional poker players respect Johnny Chan, the player and the man. And this includes Phil Hellmuth Jr. Another World Series of Poker champion, T. J. Cloutier, says that Johnny reads opponents better than anyone else. That's part of what makes Johnny a champion.

"Chip Reese. He's like a mentor to me. He's got everything. He's cool, he's the best all-round player there is, he takes care of himself. Everything he does is just the right thing to do. That's all I want to do in life—do the right thing every time."

The love flows both ways. Most professional players (even Phil Hellmuth) have only good to say about Johnny Chan. Steve Hirano quotes T. J. Cloutier, another famous player and Hall of Fame member, in his Goldsea.com article. T. J.'s statements are typical of how people feel about Johnny:

> **"As far as I'm concerned, Johnny's always the favorite to win the World Series. He's the best at reading other players. At least 90 percent of the time he's right."**

When Johnny entered the poker world, he was the only Asian on the circuit. That is no longer true. Men "the Master" Nguyen has won over seventy-five major tournaments. He's earned six gold bracelets as well, making him one of the most successful players on the circuit. Like Johnny, he also mentors the next generation of players.

The One, the Only

High-stakes poker today is a different world from the one Johnny entered thirty years ago. The fields are bigger, the games are harder, the competition is tougher, and the glory is greater. Furthermore, when Johnny Chan began playing high-stakes poker, he was virtually the only Asian player.

Today, that too has changed. Johnny was an inspiration, and other Asian players followed. David Chiu, Chau Giang, John Juanda, Minh Ly, Tony Ma, Evelyn Ng, Men Nguyen, Scotty Nguyen, An Tran, J. C. Tran, and Mimi Tran are just a few of the poker players of Asian heritage playing professionally today.

POKER AND ASIAN PLAYERS

In an article for Hold'emShirts.net, poker superstar Daniel Negreanu made these observations about Asian poker players:

"It's very hard to ignore how successful the Asian players are in tournament poker. Of the top 20 in Card Player's Player of the Year Standings, nine are Asian. . . . So, what is it about [Asians] that makes them so good? Is it in their blood? Are they naturally smarter than people in most other cultures?

"John Juanda came up with a theory that I thought was very profound. He explained to me that when he first came to this country, he spoke little if any English. So, when he played poker, all he did was watch the action and study people's body language. If someone was talking to him, he couldn't understand what the person was saying, but based on body language and facial expressions, he would make educated guesses as to what the person was saying. John went on to say, 'You learn a lot more by listening than you do by talking.' Think about that for a moment, as I think it's a great life lesson.

"I have asked others for their opinions as to why Asians seem to do so well as a whole in poker, and have heard a wide variety of answers: 'They are hungry. They work hard because they know they have to.' 'They don't take things for granted.' 'They have a lot of heart.' All of those responses seem to be reasonable explanations, as far as I'm concerned."

Another successful Asian poker player is Evelyn "Evy" Ng of Toronto, Ontario. Along with Jennifer Harman, Annie Duke, Vera Richmond, Kathy Liebert, and others, Evy has played a role in proving to players and fans alike that poker is no longer a game just for men. The number of women on the pro circuit has grown with the game's popularity.

Johnny is happy to see so many people following in his footsteps, but he's also as egotistical as ever. Steve Hirano's article also quotes Johnny on his feelings toward the new generation of Asian players:

> **"I'm the best player in the Asian community. They're all dreaming they're going to be the Orient Express II."**

Call it arrogance, or call it honesty. But one thing is for certain. There's only one "Orient Express" in poker. The original, Johnny Chan.

CHRONOLOGY

1957   Johnny Chan is born in Guangzhou, China.

1966   Johnny's family immigrates to the United States.

1970   The first World Series of Poker (WSOP) is played at Binion's Horseshoe casino.

1973   Johnny makes his first trip to Las Vegas. He is 16 years old.

1985   Johnny wins his first WSOP bracelet.

1987   Johnny wins his first WSOP World Championship.

1988   Johnny wins his second consecutive WSOP World Championship.

1989   At age twenty-four, Phil Hellmuth Jr. beats Johnny Chan to become the youngest World Champion in history.

1995   Poker legend Johnny Moss dies.

1998   *Rounders*, starring Matt Damon and Edward Norton, premiers. Johnny makes a cameo appearance in the film.

2002   The World Poker Tour (WPT) begins; Johnny Chan is inducted into the Poker Hall of Fame.

2003   The first television broadcasts of the WPT air and become the highest-rated show in Travel Channel history; at the WSOP Doyle Brunson, Johnny Chan, and Phil Hellmuth all bring their bracelet counts to nine.

2005   Johnny becomes the first poker player to win ten WSOP bracelets. Doyle Brunson wins his tenth a few days later.

2006   Phil Hellmuth Jr. wins his tenth bracelet at the WSOP. Johnny's protégé, Jamie Gold, wins the World Championship.

ACCOMPLISHMENTS & AWARDS

World Series of Poker Wins
1985 $1000 Limit Holdem
1987 $10,000 No Limit Holdem Main Event
1988 $10,000 No Limit Holdem Main Event
1994 $1500 Seven Card Stud
1997 $5000 Deuce to Seven Draw
2000 $1500 Pot Limit Omaha
2002 $2500 No Limit Holdem Gold Bracelet Match Play
2003 $5000 No Limit Holdem; $5000 Pot Limit Omaha
2005 $2500 Pot Limit Hold'em

Other Major Tournament Wins
1982 $10,000 No Limit Hold'em, America's Cup of Poker
1983 $10,000 No Limit Hold'em, America's Cup of Poker
1985 $1000 Omaha, Amarillo Slim's Superbowl of Poker
1987 $10,000 No Limit Hold'em, 3rd Annual Diamond Jim Brady
1988 $5000 Championship Event—No Limit Hold'em, Hall of Fame Poker Classic
1989 $5000 Championship Event—No Limit Hold'em, Hall of Fame Poker Classic

Filmography
1998 *Rounders*, starring Matt Damon and Edward Norton (cameo appearance)

2007 *Lucky You*, starring Eric Bana, Drew Barrymore, and Robert Duvall (cameo appearance)

Publications
2005 Chan, Johnny, and Mark Karowe. *Play Poker Like Johnny Chan, Book One: Casino Poker*. Santa Ana, Calif.: Seven Locks Press.

2006 Chan, Johnny, and Mark Karowe. *Million Dollar Hold'em: Limit Cash Games*. New York: Cardoza.

FURTHER READING & INTERNET RESOURCES

Books

Ackerman, Loren, and Christopher Ackerman. *Talkin' About Poker: Straight Talk for Parents and Their Players.* Hackettstown, N.J.: High Powered Publishing LLC, 2006.

Craig, Michael. *The Professor, the Banker, and the Suicide King: Inside the Richest Poker Game of All Time.* New York: Warner Books, 2005.

Fornatale, Peter. *Winning Secrets of Poker.* New York: DRF Press, 2006.

Kaplan, Michael, and Brad Reagan. *Aces and Kings: Inside Stories and Million Dollar Strategies from Poker's Greatest Players.* New York: Wenner Books, 2006.

Nosek, Jude. *Poker Night Handbook: A Guide for Getting a Game Together and Keeping It Fun and Exciting.* Oak Park, Ill.: KnackPacks, 2002.

Web Sites

www.allinmag.com
All In

www.bluffmagazine.com
Bluff

www.cardplayer.com
Card Player

www.chanpoker.com
Johnny Chan's Official Web Site

www.pokerpages.com
Poker Pages.com

www.worldpokertour.com
World Poker Tour

GLOSSARY

binge—A short period during which someone eats or drinks much more than someone ordinarily would during the same time.

coveted—Wanted something very much.

elite—A small group of people within a larger group who have more power, social standing, wealth, or talent than the rest of the group.

feigned—Faked.

icon—Someone widely admired as a symbol of a field of activity.

immortalized—Made someone's memory live on.

inducted—Formally admitted into an organization.

intimidation—The act of persuading someone to do something or dissuading someone from doing something through the use of fear tactics.

legitimacy—Legality.

neuropsychologist—Someone who studies the branch of neurology that deals with behavior.

piqued—Aroused interest.

protégé—Someone who receives help and guidance from a person who is more experienced.

scenarios—Imagined sequences of possible events.

stagnant—Not making progress.

SELECT POKER TERMS

All-in—When you have put all of your playable money and chips into the pot during the course of a hand.

Ante—A prescribed amount posted before the start of a hand by all players.

Bet—The act of placing a wager in turn into the pot on any betting round, or the chips put into the pot.

Big blind—The largest regular blind in a game.

Blind—A required bet made before any cards are dealt.

Bluff—A bet or raise with a hand that is unlikely to beat the other players.

Board card—A community card in the center of the table, as in Hold'em or Omaha.

Button—A player who is in the designated dealer position.

Buy-in—The minimum amount of money required to enter any game.

Check—To waive the right to initiate the betting in a round.

Check-raise—To waive the right to bet until a bet has been made by an opponent, and then to increase the bet by at least an equal amount when it is your turn to act.

Community cards—The cards dealt face up in the center of the table that can be used by all players to form their best hand in the games of Hold'em and Omaha.

Cut—To divide the deck into two sections in such a manner as to change the order of the cards.

Discards(s)—In a draw game, the card(s) thrown away; the muck.

Face card—A king, queen, or jack.

Fixed limit—In limit poker, any betting structure in which the amount of the bet on each particular round is pre-set.

Flop—In Hold'em or Omaha, the three community cards that are turned simultaneously after the first round of betting.

Fold—To throw a hand away and relinquish all interest in a pot.

Heads-up play—Only two players involved in play.

Kicker—The highest unpaired card that helps determine the value of a five-card poker hand.

Loose—Playing more hands than normal.

Muck—(1) The pile of discards gathered facedown in the center of the table by the dealer; (2) To discard a hand.

Over card—A hole card that is higher than any other card on the board.

Play the board—Using all five community cards for your hand in Hold'em.

Pot-limit—The betting structure of a game in which you are allowed to bet up to the amount of the pot.

Raise—To increase the amount of a previous wager.

River—The final card dealt.

Showdown—The final act of determining the winner of the pot after all betting has been completed.

Small blind—In a game with multiple blind bets, the smallest blind.

Split pot—A pot that is divided among players, either because of a tie for the best hand or by agreement prior to the showdown.

Suited—Cards are of the same suit.

Tight—Playing fewer hands than normal.

Tight game—A game with less players than normal in fewer hands.

Turn—The fourth card dealt on the board during community card games.

Select Poker Slang

All blue—A flush containing either clubs or spades.

All pink—A flush containing either diamonds or hearts.

Back door—Making a hand that the player wasn't drawing at.

Bad beat—A hand being beat by another hand that had a very low percentage of becoming a winning hand.

Cards speak—The face value of a hand in a showdown is the true value of the hand, regardless of a verbal announcement.

Drawing dead—Drawing to a hand that cannot win because someone already holds a hand that will beat what you are drawing to.

Potting out—Agreeing with another player to take money out of a pot, often to buy food, cigarettes, or drinks, or to make side bets.

Rags—Cards generally not worth playing.

Dolly Parton—A hand containing a 9 and a 5.

Rocket cards—Two aces.

Jackson 5—Jack and a five.

Pocket rockets—Two aces dealt face down.

Big slick—Ace and a king.

Ducks—Two 2s.

Paint—Any face card.

Rainbow—Three or four cards of different suits.

Nuts—The best possible hand.

Texas Hold'em Hand Rankings

The top ten Texas Hold'em hands in descending order of rank and the odds of seeing one when playing Texas Hold'em poker.

1 ROYAL FLUSH

A♠ K♠ Q♠ J♠ 10♠

A Ten-to-Ace straight, all in one suit
Odds against getting one: 30,939-to-1

2 STRAIGHT FLUSH

Q♦ J♦ 10♦ 9♦ 8♦

A run of five card values, all in one suit
Odds against getting one: 3,590-to-1

3 FOUR OF A KIND

7♦ 7♣ 7♥ 7♠ K♥

All four cards of the same value
Odds against getting one: 594-to-1

4 FULL HOUSE

9♦ 9♣ 9♠ J♦ J♥

Three of a kind, plus a pair (any suits)
Odds against getting one: 37.5-to-1

5 FLUSH

K♥ J♥ 8♥ 5♥ 3♥

Five cards (any values) in the same suit
Odds against getting one: 32.1-to-1

6 STRAIGHT

A♣ 2♦ 3♥ 4♣ 5♠

A run of five card values, in any suits
Odds against getting one: 20.6-to-1

7 THREE OF A KIND

4♣ 4♥ 4♠ 6♠ Q♥

Three cards of the same value
Odds against getting one: 19.7-to-1

8 TWO PAIR

10♣ 10♦ K♠ K♦ 2♣

Two sets of two cards of the same value
Odds against getting one: 3.26-to-1

9 ONE PAIR

5♣ 5♦ 6♥ A♠ 9♣

Two cards of the same value
Odds against getting one: 1.28-to-1

10 HIGH CARD ONLY

A♥ 10♣ 9♦ 5♠ 3♥

A hand with no pairs, straight, or flush
Odds against getting one: 4.74-to-1

INDEX

About the Author

Mitch Roycroft is a professional children's writer who has written numerous books and articles for young people. Mitch has lived in the United States, Canada, and Africa, currently resides in Toronto, Ontario, and is contemplating a move to Europe. Mitch enjoys playing poker, but he doesn't like to play for money.

Picture Credits